W9-CIA-974

US SPECIAL FORCES

NAVY SEALS

By Drew Nelson

Gareth Stevens
Publishing

Please visit our website, www.garethstevens.com. For a free color catalog of all our high-quality books, call toll free 1-800-542-2595 or fax 1-877-542-2596.

Library of Congress Cataloging-in-Publication Data

Nelson, Drew, 1986-
Navy SEALs / Drew Nelson.
    p. cm. — (US Special Forces)
Includes index.
ISBN 978-1-4339-6567-8 (pbk.)
ISBN 978-1-4339-6568-5 (6-pack)
ISBN 978-1-4339-6565-4 (library binding)
1. United States. Navy. SEALs—Juvenile literature. 2. United States. Navy—Commando troops—Juvenile literature. I. Title.
VG87.N45 2012
359.9′84—dc23

2011026009

First Edition

Published in 2012 by
Gareth Stevens Publishing
111 East 14th Street, Suite 349
New York, NY 10003

Copyright © 2012 Gareth Stevens Publishing

Designer: Michael J. Flynn
Editor: Kristen Rajczak

Photo credits: Cover, p. 1 MILpictures by Tom Weber; photos courtesy of US Navy: pp. 4 by Brandan W. Schulze, 5 by Adam Henderson, 9 by Joshua T. Rodriguez, 10, 11 by Andrew McKaskle, 13 by William S. Parker, 14 by Tim Turner, 15, 18–19 by Gary L. Johnson III, 20 by Shauntae Hinkle-Lymas, 21 by John Scorza, 22–23 by Eric S. Logsdon, 25 by Monsoor family, 27 by Lance Cpl. Ryan Rholes, 28–29 by Jayme Pastoric; pp. 6–7 W. Eugene Smith/Time & Life Pictures/Getty Images; p. 8 US Navy/Archive Photos/Getty Images; pp. 16–17 Gilles Bassignac/Gamma-Rapho/Getty Images; p. 24 Andy Lyons/Getty Images.

Printed in the United States of America

CPSIA compliance information: Batch #CW12GS: For further information contact Gareth Stevens, New York, New York at 1-800-542-2595.

CONTENTS

Words in the glossary appear in **bold** type the first time they are used in the text.

WHO ARE THE NAVY SEALS?

The US Navy SEALs are sailors who are trained to carry out special **missions** and secret operations all over the world. Their name comes from all the different kinds of places they can work. "SEAL" stands for "**SE**a, **A**ir, and **L**and." SEALs are part of a division of the navy called the Naval Special Warfare community.

The SEAL Trident

All SEALs wear the Special Warfare **Insignia**. It's also called the SEAL Trident and has been nicknamed "the Budweiser."

A person wearing the Trident has passed SEAL training—called Basic Underwater **Demolition**/SEAL school, or BUD/S—and become a SEAL.

The SEALs' job is to keep the United States safe. Many times, they work quietly and at night to carry out their missions in secret. They're always **deployed** around the world in small, well-trained teams to carry out important tasks.

These SEALs are practicing how to board an oil platform from a moving boat.

BEFORE THERE WERE SEALS

Many other kinds of special land and sea forces existed before the SEALs. In 1942, during World War II, the army and navy started jointly training a beach **reconnaissance** force called the Scouts and Raiders. Their job was to secretly go to a beach before the rest of the soldiers got there. The Scouts and Raiders figured out enemy positions and planned attacks.

In 1943, the navy created the Underwater Demolition Teams (UDTs). These special groups wore swimsuits, fins, and facemasks, and were trained to plant bombs on enemy targets underwater.

US soldiers scout a beach in Japan during World War II.

Other Early Navy Special Forces

Naval **Combat** Demolition Units: These World War II sailors trained in both beach and above-water explosives.

Office of **Strategic** Services Operational Swimmers: These men trained to swim into and out of enemy waters on reconnaissance and combat missions.

HISTORY OF THE SEALS

In 1961, President John F. Kennedy asked the military to form a new team of soldiers that could carry out secret operations in or near rivers and oceans. He wanted a Special Forces group that could complete unusual missions. In January 1962, the US Navy formed SEAL Teams One and Two. These two teams were made up of members of Underwater Demolition Teams.

Navy SEALs prepare for combat in South Vietnam in 1967.

The first war the navy SEALs fought in was the **Vietnam r**. At first, they just gave advice to other members of the tary. In February 1966, the SEALs started their first ive missions.

The Bull Frog

The active-duty SEAL who's served the longest is given the title of "Bull Frog." He also gets a trophy to display for the entire time he's the Bull Frog. Pictured below, former Bull Frogs pass the trophy around during the Bull Frog ceremony in 2009.

AFTER THE VIETNAM WAR

Many SEALs stayed in Vietnam after the United States left the war. They gave advice to the military there until 1973. Then, in May 1983, all members of the Underwater Demolition Teams became navy SEALs or part of the Swimmer Delivery **Vehicle** Teams (SDVTs). The SDVTs, now called SEAL Delivery Vehicle Teams, get the SEALs where they need to be.

Between 1983 and 1991, the SEALs carried out missions all over the world. They took part in Operation Urgent Fury in Grenada, Operation Earnest Will in the Persian Gulf, Operation Just Cause in Panama, and Operation Desert Storm in the Persian Gulf.

This photo of SEAL Team Four was taken just before Operation Just Cause.

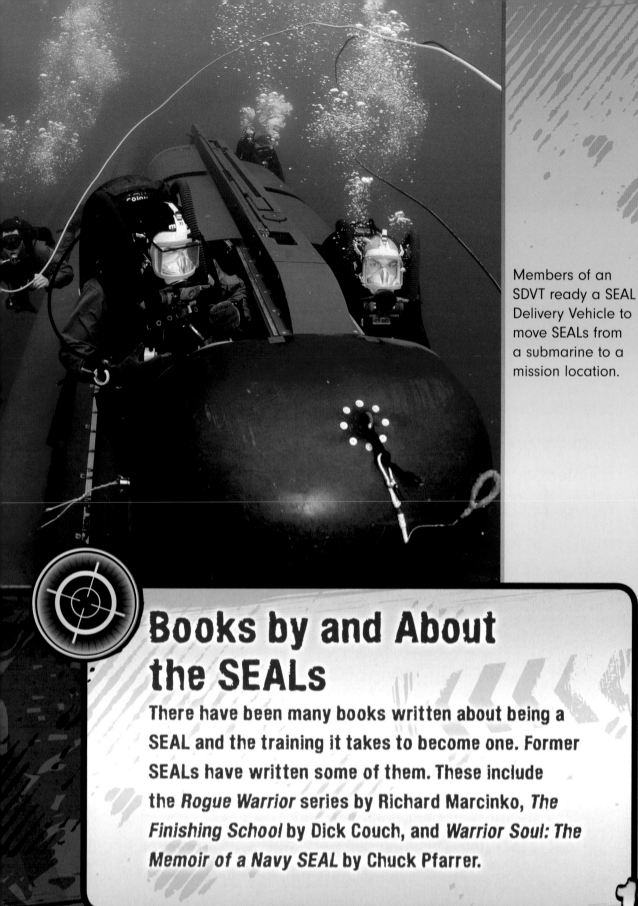

Members of an SDVT ready a SEAL Delivery Vehicle to move SEALs from a submarine to a mission location.

Books by and About the SEALs

There have been many books written about being a SEAL and the training it takes to become one. Former SEALs have written some of them. These include the *Rogue Warrior* series by Richard Marcinko, *The Finishing School* by Dick Couch, and *Warrior Soul: The Memoir of a Navy SEAL* by Chuck Pfarrer.

TYPES OF SEAL MISSIONS

There are four main kinds of missions the SEALs carry out. They are direct action, special reconnaissance, counterterrorism, and foreign internal defense.

In direct action, SEALs attack enemy targets. In special reconnaissance missions, SEALs sneak into enemy territory and find out information, such as where the enemies are, what they're doing, and what kind of forces they have. In counterterrorism, the SEALs follow the activities of **terrorist** groups and act directly against them to prevent terrorist attacks. In foreign internal defense, the SEALs train and help soldiers in other countries act when their enemies attack.

Gear for Every Mission

The SEALs must be prepared for any type of mission at sea, in the air, or on land. To do this, they use a wide variety of gear meant to help them in each kind of location. This includes parachutes, night-vision goggles, and small inflatable boats called Zodiacs.

This navy SEAL is training for combat aboard a ship. SEALs take part in training like this throughout their time in the military.

13

OPERATIONS OF FREEDOM

After the terrorist attacks against the United States on September 11, 2001, the US Navy SEALs were sent into Afghanistan. In fact, the first high-ranking officer in Afghanistan after military operations began was a navy SEAL!

The mission in Afghanistan was called Operation Enduring Freedom. The SEALs and other Special Forces completed more than 75 special reconnaissance and direct action missions. This included searching for terrorists trying to leave the country and getting rid of more than 500,000 pounds (227,000 kg) of weapons and explosives. As of 2011, some SEALs were still taking part in Operation Enduring Freedom.

A navy SEAL takes part in a mission in Afghanistan in 2002.

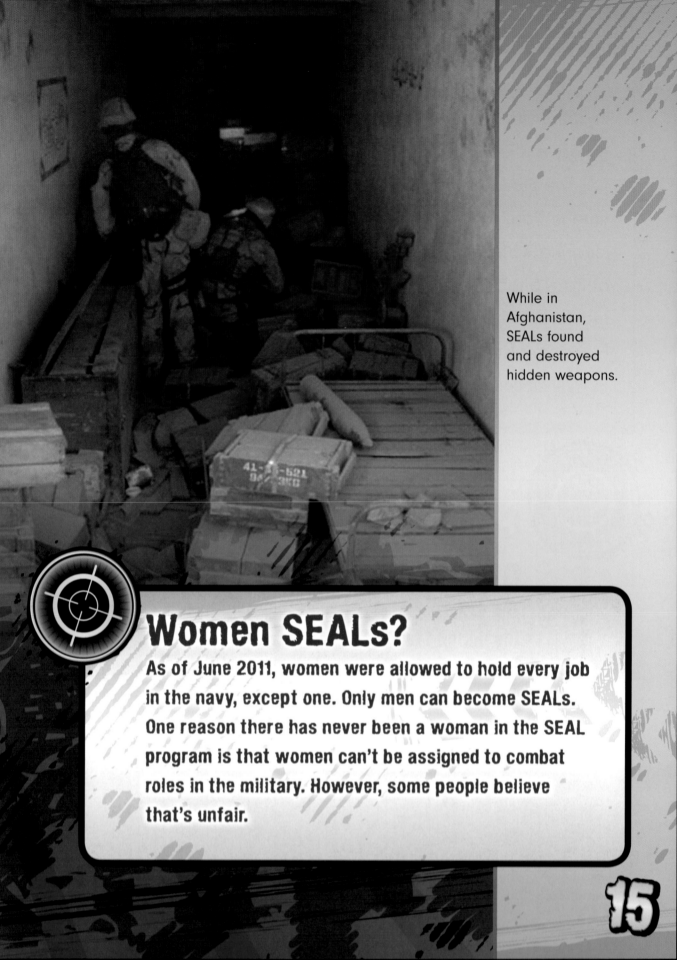

While in Afghanistan, SEALs found and destroyed hidden weapons.

Women SEALs?

As of June 2011, women were allowed to hold every job in the navy, except one. Only men can become SEALs. One reason there has never been a woman in the SEAL program is that women can't be assigned to combat roles in the military. However, some people believe that's unfair.

The SEALs began taking part in Operation Iraqi Freedom in 2003. This mission used more SEALs than any other in the history of the Naval Special Warfare group.

The SEALs carried out many different actions during their time in Iraq. These include securing places that produced oil, clearing waterways to allow the transport of aid to the people of Iraq, attacking possible terrorist locations, and capturing most-wanted enemies. The SEALs fighting in Operation Iraqi Freedom also conducted the first rescue of prisoners of war, or POWs, since World War II.

Congressional Medal of Honor

The Congressional Medal of Honor is the highest award the United States gives for bravery. Three SEALs have received this award for acts of courage: Lieutenants Joseph Robert Kerrey and Michael Murphy, and Petty Officer 2nd Class Michael A. Monsoor.

SEALs were part of the US troops who forced Saddam Hussein, Iraq's president, out of power in Iraq. Here, soldiers pull down a statue of him.

17

SEAL TEAM LOCATIONS

SEAL teams are based at three US Duty Stations. The commanders are located in Coronado, California. The group that runs SEAL training is also there, as well as SEAL Teams One, Three, Five, and Seven. SEAL Team Seventeen, a reserve unit composed of sailors not on active duty, is there, too.

Little Creek, Virginia, is home to SEAL Teams Two, Four, Eight, and Ten, as well as the reserve unit SEAL Team Eighteen. SEAL Team Six is located in nearby Virginia Beach. The third Duty Station is in Pearl Harbor, Hawaii. The SEAL Delivery Vehicle Team, the group that helps the SEALs travel, is located there.

Little Creek, Virginia
Virginia Beach, Virginia

Coronado, California

Pearl Harbor, Hawaii

There seem to be nine SEAL teams plus the reserves. However, the military doesn't back up that number or the existence of SEAL Team Nine.

Special Warfare Combatant-craft Crewmen (SWCC)

The Special Warfare Combatant-craft Crewmen are the highly trained sailors who operate and take care of the boats and vehicles the SEALs use to get to and from their targets. They drive high-speed boats and are trained to use many state-of-the-art weapons.

TRAINING TO BE A SEAL

Training to be a SEAL is considered the hardest military training there is. It lasts for at least 2 1/2 years!

First, trainees must go to SEAL Prep School and take a difficult fitness test. In the school, they train to improve their test performance for an even harder fitness test they must complete in order to continue with SEAL training. If they pass this second test, trainees enter BUD/S school, a 24-week program that teaches **stamina** and leadership skills. There, they have three different training sessions. Each takes 7 weeks and includes physical conditioning, combat diving, and land warfare.

SEAL candidates carry a boat during BUD/S School.

Qualifications for SEAL Training

In order to enter SEAL training, a candidate must be able to complete the following test:

- Swim 500 yards (457.2 m) in 12 minutes, 30 seconds

- Rest 10 minutes

- Do 42 push-ups in 2 minutes

- Rest 2 minutes

- Do 50 sit-ups in 2 minutes

- Rest 2 minutes

- Do 6 pull-ups with no time limit

- Rest 10 minutes

- Run 1.5 miles (2.4 km) in 11 minutes

SEAL candidates train during BUD/S School in 2010.

21

After completing BUD/S school, trainees go to a 3-week session of Parachute Jump School, where they're trained to jump from planes. Once this is finished, they go into SEAL Qualification Training, a 26-week program at the Duty Station at Coronado. There, trainees learn skills specific to the SEALs and their missions, including how to endure cold water, sea operations, combat swimming, and how to fight in small spaces.

After trainees have graduated from SEAL Qualification Training, they spend 18 months taking part in advanced training for different positions, such as medical officers. Some SEALs learn how to speak other languages, become **snipers**, or use **tactical** communications.

A group of navy SEALs take part in Advanced Cold Weather training.

Qualifications to Apply to the SEAL Program

Before they can start training, SEAL candidates must meet these qualifications:

- Have excellent eyesight

- Score high enough on a special military job test

- Be no more than 28 years old

- Be a US citizen

- Pass the physical exam for diving

23

NOTABLE NAVY SEALS

Many SEALs have gone on to become famous after leaving the military. Former SEAL Jesse Ventura became a professional wrestler known as "The Body." He later became an actor, and in 1998, he became the governor of Minnesota.

Rudy Boesch was on the first season of the TV show *Survivor* and finished in third place. Former SEALs Harry Humphries and Chuck Pfarrer work in the movie business, giving advice and writing. Both Dick Couch and Richard Marcinko went on to become famous authors. Two former SEALs, William M. Shepherd and Chris Cassidy, even became astronauts and went into space!

Jesse Ventura sports his military pride on a navy SEAL hat in 2002.

Michael A. Monsoor, shown here, was awarded the Medal of Honor after he died saving his teammates from a grenade.

Silver Screen SEALs

There have been a number of movies featuring navy SEALs. One from 1990 is called *Navy SEALs*. It stars Charlie Sheen and was written by former SEAL Chuck Pfarrer. Other movies include *Tears of the Sun*, *Shadow Warriors*, and *Behind Enemy Lines II*.

THE PROUD BUT FEW

While there have been many SEALs since the beginning of the program in 1962, there are very few at any one time. There are only about 2,500 working SEALs in the world right now.

Also, while about 1,000 men begin SEAL training at the BUD/S school every year, only between 200 and 250 complete the training and become SEALs. People who enter the school but can't complete it on the first try are given a different job with the navy. They're allowed to apply again after 2 years.

Homework for SEAL School

While very few people complete SEAL training, there's a workout plan that the navy gives to every person entering training to prepare them for the difficult BUD/S school. The Physical Training Guide includes 26 weeks of daily running, swimming, and weight training.

These navy SEALs are some of the most skilled sailors in the world.

MODERN MISSIONS AND THE FUTURE

In early May 2011, SEAL Team Six completed Operation Neptune Spear. This was the secret mission to capture or kill Osama bin Laden, the leader of the group that carried out the terrorist attacks in the United States in 2001. This successful operation by the navy SEALs ended almost a decade of searching for bin Laden.

SEAL Team Six's success in Operation Neptune Spear made SEALs like these better known all over the world.

The US Navy SEALs will continue to carry out special missions at sea, in the air, and on land for years to come. They operate secretly all over the world to make sure all Americans are safe.

The SEAL Ethos

There is a special code that all SEALs follow in life. This is called the SEAL Ethos. In this code, SEALs promise to be loyal, never quit, serve with honor, and stop America's enemies.

GLOSSARY

combat: armed fighting between opposing forces

demolition: the act of working with explosives to destroy things

deploy: to move troops into a position of readiness

insignia: a mark on a uniform that shows honor

mission: a task or job a group must perform

reconnaissance: a search for useful information

sniper: a soldier specially trained to shoot well from a hiding place

stamina: able to do something hard for a long time

strategic: having to do with the use of a clever plan or skill

tactical: having to do with a method for accomplishing a military goal

terrorist: having to do with the use of violence and fear to challenge an authority

vehicle: an object used for carrying or transporting people or goods, such as a car, truck, or airplane

Vietnam War: a conflict starting in 1957 and ending in 1975 between South Vietnam and North Vietnam in which the United States joined with South Vietnam

FOR MORE INFORMATION

Books

Hamilton, John. *Navy SEALs*. Edina, MN: ABDO Publishing Company, 2012.

Hunter, Nick. *Military Survival*. Chicago, IL: Raintree Publishing, 2011.

Yomtov, Nelson. *Navy SEALs in Action*. New York, NY: Bearport Publishing, 2008.

Websites

Navy SEALs (Sea, Air & Land)
www.navy.com/navy/careers/special-operations/seals/
Learn more about the SEALs' job and how to become a SEAL.

US Navy SEALs
www.sealswcc.com
Read about SEALs history, training, and what they are doing today.

INDEX